HEALTHY WEIGHT GAIN:

The Complete Guide to Transform Your Body from Skinny to Strong And Add Weight With Nutritious Meals.

Copyright

Healthy Weight Gain

Table of Contents

Healthy Weight Gain

INTRODUCTION

Let me tell you the story of a woman called Maddie:

Maddie had always been on the thin side; she was often tired and had little energy. Time and time again, she tried to embark on a weight gain program but never saw results. It was difficult to gain weight, yet easy to lose any pound that mistakenly stayed. Of course, this doesn't mean she didn't have a positive image of her body, she did, but has always been on the underweight end of the BMI scale all her adult life. Even though she was petite and confident in her own skin, being underweight is still unhealthy. She decided it was time to make a change: pack on a few pounds and get her body in balance. At the time, her weight ranged between 94-99lbs to a 5.6" height.

She spent time researching how weight works, learning about nutrition, experimenting with foods and starting a healthy diet. She also learned about the importance of regular exercise for gaining muscle and maintaining a healthy weight. Maddie began to incorporate healthy, nutritious foods into her diet and gradually increased her calorie intake. She made sure to include plenty of proteins, fruits, vegetables, and healthy fats- the goal is to gain a healthy weight.

Gradually, Maddie began to see results, both in her body and in her mind. She felt stronger and more energized than ever before, and her confidence grew as she saw the positive changes in her body and mind. People started noticing too, and the compliments always made her feel warm.
Her efforts had paid off!

The first time she saw 135lbs on the weight scale, she couldn't help screaming. She had gained weight! Healthy weight! Her BMI now sits pretty in the healthy range. She was thrilled with her accomplishment and felt empowered knowing she had taken control of her health.
Maddie realized that her journey to a healthy weight wasn't just about her body, but about her overall well-being. She had learned to value herself, and her newfound confidence and self-love were contagious. She shared her story with others who were struggling with similar issues and became a source of inspiration for those who wanted to make positive changes in their own lives.

Healthy Weight Gain

She now uses the skills she learned to maintain her healthy weight and has helped many other 'skinny people' to gain weight, healthily.

The woman in this story is me.

I know all the struggles associated with weight gain. People tell you to just eat more, but they haven't been there and may not understand when you say you are full. After all, I can't eat more than my stomach can take. What about the war against lack of appetite? Oh! It is also possible to actually eat MORE, and not add the desired weight, instead, you upset your stomach.

I have been through it all.

A lot of attention is placed on weight loss, there's an abundance of tips and resources on that. But a lot of people (like me) also struggle to gain weight, yet not many people see us. Being underweight can negatively impact one's physical and mental health, leading to a host of health problems and concerns.

Healthy Weight Gain

This book is designed to provide a comprehensive guide to gaining weight (as an underweight person or low range healthy weight), including information on body mass index (BMI), nutrition, exercise, and lifestyle factors.

Gaining healthy weight is a challenge, but it doesn't have to be. In this book, you will find practical and easy-to-follow advice on how to gain weight in a healthy way. We'll look at the different types of foods that can help you to gain weight, how to prepare them, as well as the importance of exercise and lifestyle changes.

This book is designed to provide you with the actionable steps and knowledge to help your journey. From understanding your body's needs to creating a plan that works for you, you'll have the right strategies to gain healthy weight and reach your goals in no time!

Whether you are trying to break free from anorexia, or to attain a body goal and just be healthier, I am not asking you to do anything out of the ordinary. My method is as simple as E.S.E Eat-Sleep-Exercise. I didn't have to eat out of compulsion, I also never step foot into the gym.

The E.S.E model worked for me and I've seen it work for many other people I shared the good news with.

Now, it's your turn…

CHAPTER 1

HOW WEIGHT GAIN WORKS

The truth is weight gain can be done either healthily, or unhealthily.

Healthy weight gain refers to the intentional increase in body weight that is achieved through a combination of proper nutrition and regular exercise. The keyword here is INTENTIONAL. It is the process of gaining weight in a manner that promotes optimal health and wellness, rather than simply increasing body fat or body mass index (BMI) without regard to overall health. You are not trying to be fat; you are working to be healthy. You want to give your body balance and strengthen it, healthily.

Healthy weight gain requires a calorie surplus, which means consuming more calories than the body burns through physical activity and metabolism. However, the quality of these calories is important. Many people think that gaining weight is as simple as eating more calories, but the truth is that healthy weight gain is a bit more complicated than that. A healthy weight gain diet should be rich in nutrient-dense foods such as whole grains, lean proteins, fruits, vegetables, and healthy fats. These foods provide the necessary macronutrients (protein, carbohydrates, and fats) and micronutrients (vitamins and minerals) needed for optimal health and muscle growth.

How Important is Nutrition?

Nutrition plays a critical role in gaining weight as an underweight person. Eating a diet rich in calories and nutrients is essential to support healthy weight gain. This includes consuming adequate amounts of protein, carbohydrates, and healthy fats.

Protein is particularly important for building and repairing muscle tissue, which can help increase body weight. Good sources of protein include lean meats, poultry, fish, eggs, beans, and nuts.

Carbohydrates provide the body with energy, which is necessary for physical activity and overall health. Complex carbohydrates, such as whole grains, fruits, and vegetables, are preferred over simple carbohydrates, such as sugary snacks and drinks.

Healthy fats, such as those found in avocados, nuts, and olive oil, can also help promote healthy weight gain. These fats provide essential nutrients and help the body absorb fat-soluble vitamins.

Metabolism and Metabolic Rate

Metabolism is a complex biochemical process that occurs within the body and is responsible for many of our bodily functions. It converts the food we eat into energy and is responsible for our weight gain or loss. Metabolism is a major factor when it comes to weight gain, and understanding its effects is important when it comes to making healthy lifestyle choices.

The metabolic rate of an individual is determined by the amount of energy that is used by the body for essential bodily functions such as breathing, digestion, and circulation. Metabolic rate is measured in calories, and it can vary widely from person to person.

For most naturally petite people, we have a higher metabolic rate and burn more calories than people who are naturally chubby. Metabolic rate is a key factor why you are not gaining the desired weight.

Vitamins and minerals play an important role in supporting overall health and wellness, including healthy weight gain. While they don't provide calories like macronutrients do, vitamins and minerals are essential for various metabolic processes in the body, including energy production and muscle growth.

Some key vitamins and minerals for healthy weight gain include:

Vitamin D: Vitamin D is important for bone health and immune function, but it also plays a role in muscle function and growth. Research has shown that vitamin D deficiency may be linked to muscle weakness and decreased muscle mass. Good sources of vitamin D include fatty fish, egg yolks, and fortified foods such as milk and cereal.

Calcium: Calcium is important for bone health, but it also plays a role in muscle contraction and energy metabolism. Good sources of calcium include dairy products, leafy green vegetables, and fortified foods.

Iron: Iron is important for energy production and oxygen transport throughout the body. Iron deficiency can lead to fatigue and decreased muscle function. Good sources of iron include lean meats, poultry, fish, and plant-based sources such as beans and spinach.

Magnesium: Magnesium is important for energy metabolism and muscle function. It also plays a role in regulating blood sugar levels and blood pressure. Good sources of magnesium include nuts, seeds, whole grains, and leafy green vegetables.

B vitamins: B vitamins, including thiamin, riboflavin, niacin, and vitamin B12, play a role in energy production and metabolism. They are also important for nerve and muscle function. Good sources of B vitamins include whole grains, lean meats, fish, and fortified foods.

It is important to consume adequate amounts of vitamins and minerals for overall health. While some of these have been made available in forms of supplements, it's also important to avoid excessive supplementation, as high doses of certain vitamins and minerals can be harmful. I personally recommend food, but I've also worked with people who use supplements (for health reasons, to boost appetite, etc.).

Calorie Intake

Calorie intake is a crucial factor when it comes to weight gain. It refers to the amount of energy that is consumed through food and beverages. When you consume more calories than your body needs, the excess energy is stored as fat, which can lead to weight gain over time. To gain weight, you need to consume more calories than you burn daily. This is known as a calorie surplus. A calorie surplus of 500-1000 calories per day is generally recommended.

I should also mention that *not all calories are created equal.* The source of your calories can have a significant impact on your overall health and body composition. This is why I emphasize nutrient-dense, calorie-rich foods such as whole grains, lean proteins, healthy fats, and fruits and vegetables to support your weight gain goals.

Macronutrients And Weight Gain

It sounds like science, I know, but it is key to understand the science of nutrition in order to be able to make it work for your body.

Macronutrients are nutrients that the body requires in large amounts to support various functions, including growth, energy production, and muscle building. There are three primary macronutrients: carbohydrates, proteins, and fats. Each macronutrient plays a unique role in the body, and understanding how they work together can be beneficial for weight gain.

Carbohydrates are the body's primary source of energy. They are broken down into glucose, which is then used by the body for fuel. When consumed in excess, carbohydrates can be stored as glycogen in the muscles and liver or converted to fat for later use. To support weight gain, it's important to consume complex carbohydrates such as whole grains, fruits, and vegetables, which provide fiber and other important nutrients in addition to energy.

Proteins are essential for muscle growth and repair. They are made up of amino acids, which are the building blocks of muscle tissue. Consuming adequate amounts of protein is important for weight gain, as it can support muscle growth and prevent muscle breakdown. Good sources of protein include lean meats, poultry, fish, eggs, dairy, and plant-based sources such as beans, lentils, and tofu.

Fats are an important source of energy and help to support hormone production and cell function. While consuming too much fat can contribute to weight gain, consuming healthy fats in moderation can be beneficial for overall health and weight gain. Good sources of healthy fats include nuts, seeds, avocado, fatty fish, and olive oil.

To support healthy weight gain, it's important to consume a balanced diet that includes all three macronutrients in the appropriate proportions. A diet that is too low in any one macronutrient can lead to nutrient deficiencies or imbalances, which can negatively impact weight gain efforts.

Body Mass Index (BMI)

Body mass index, or BMI, is a commonly used tool to measure an individual's body fat based on their height and weight. BMI is calculated by dividing a person's weight (in kilograms) by their height (in meters) squared. A BMI below 18.5 is considered underweight, while a BMI between 18.5 and 24.9 is considered healthy. Individuals with a BMI between 25 and 29.9 are considered overweight, and those with a BMI of 30 or higher are considered obese. While BMI is not a perfect measure of health and does not account for factors such as muscle mass, it can provide a rough estimate of whether an individual is underweight, healthy, overweight, or obese.

Benefits of healthy weight gain

Here are some potential benefits of healthy weight gain:

1. Improved muscle mass: Weight gain can result in an increase in muscle mass, which can improve strength and physical performance.

2. Increased energy levels: With weight gain, your body may have more energy stores to draw from, which can lead to increased energy levels and improved stamina.

3. Improved immune function: healthy weight gain may improve immune function and reduce the risk of infections.

4. Reduced risk of osteoporosis: Weight gain can increase bone density, reducing the risk of osteoporosis and fractures.

5. Improved mental health: For some individuals, weight gain may improve self-esteem and body image, leading to improved mental health.

6. Increased fertility: Healthy weight gain can improve fertility in both men and women by regulating hormone levels

7. Reduced risk of malnutrition: For individuals who are underweight or have a low body mass index (BMI), healthy weight gain can reduce the risk of malnutrition and nutrient deficiencies.

How To Use This Recipe Book To Achieve Your Weight Gain Goals

Here are some tips to help you get the most out of this recipe book:

- ✓ Choose recipes that are high in protein, carbohydrates, and healthy fats. These macronutrients are essential for building muscle and supporting overall health.

✓ Incorporate a variety of foods and recipes to keep your meals interesting and satisfying.

✓ Plan your meals and snacks in advance to ensure that you're consuming enough calories and nutrients each day.

✓ Use the meal planning and preparation tips provided in this book to make mealtime easier and more efficient.

✓ Be consistent with your eating habits and exercise routine to achieve the best results.

✓ Remember, healthy weight gain is a gradual process that requires patience and consistency. Don't expect to see results overnight, but with the help of this recipe book and a commitment to a healthy lifestyle, you can achieve your weight gain goals and improve your overall health and well-being.

CHAPTER 2

EATING FOR HEALTHY WEIGHT GAIN

Here are some nutrition basics for healthy weight gain:

1. Eat more calories than you burn: To gain weight, you need to consume more calories than you burn. A general rule of thumb is to consume 500-1000 calories more than your daily maintenance level.

2. Focus on nutrient-dense foods: Instead of relying on junk food or processed snacks, focus on nutrient-dense foods that provide a good balance of macronutrients (carbohydrates, proteins, and fats) and micronutrients (vitamins and minerals). Examples include whole grains, lean proteins, fruits, vegetables, nuts, and seeds. Bread is your friend on this journey, nuts and milk love you too (unless you are allergic).

3. Increase your protein intake: Protein is essential for building and repairing muscle tissue and you need it especially, since this includes exercising. Aim to consume at least 1 gram of protein per pound of body weight per day.

4. Incorporate healthy fats: Healthy fats such as avocados, nuts, seeds, and olive oil can provide a concentrated source of calories and are important for hormone production and brain function.

5. Eat frequently: The secret is not in eating monstrous amount of food at once, it is in the tiny portions that would not leave you overwhelmed. Eating frequent meals throughout the day helps you consume more calories and prevent overeating at one sitting. Aim to consume 3-4 meals per day with snacks in between, or every 2-3 hours.

6. Stay hydrated: Drinking enough water is essential for maintaining healthy bodily functions and optimal health. Aim for at least 8-10 glasses of water per day, you can also add electrolyte-rich beverages such as coconut water or sports drink to your diet.

It's time to dive into the world of healthy recipes to help you pack some healthy pounds. Are you ready?

Breakfast Recipes for Healthy Weight Gain

Banana and Oats Pancakes

This healthy breakfast option is made with mashed banana, rolled oats, eggs and milk. It is a great way to start your day with some carbs and proteins.

Ingredients

1 mashed banana,

½ cup of rolled oats,

2 eggs,

1 cup of milk,

1 teaspoon of baking powder, and

a pinch of salt.

Process

a. In a bowl, whisk together the mashed banana, rolled oats, eggs, milk and baking powder.

b. Heat a non-stick pan over medium heat and grease it lightly.

c. Pour about ¼ cup of the batter for each pancake and cook for about 2 minutes on each side.

d. Serve with your favorite toppings and enjoy!

Scrambled Eggs and Avocado Toast

This combination of scrambled eggs and avocado toast is a great way to start your day with some healthy fats and proteins.

Ingredients

2 eggs,

1 ripe avocado,

1 tablespoon of olive oil,

1 slice of whole wheat toast,

and a pinch of salt and pepper.

Process

a. Heat the olive oil in a pan over medium heat.

b. Whisk the eggs together with a pinch of salt and pepper, and then pour them into the pan.

c. Scramble the eggs until they are almost done, and then add the diced avocado to the pan.

d. Toast the slice of whole wheat bread, and then top it with the scrambled eggs and avocado.

e. Sprinkle some salt and pepper on top if desired.

f. Enjoy.

Overnight Oats

Overnight oats are a great way to enjoy a healthy and filling breakfast with fiber and healthy carbs. All you need is to soak oats in milk overnight and top with your favorite fruits or nuts for a delicious breakfast.

Ingredients

½ cup of rolled oats,

1 cup of milk,

1 tablespoon of honey,

and your favorite toppings.

Process

a. In a bowl, mix the rolled oats, milk, and honey.

b. Cover and let it sit in the refrigerator overnight.

c. In the morning, top it with your favorite fruits or nuts and enjoy.

Peanut Butter and Banana Toast

Peanut butter and banana toast is a great way to start your day with some healthy fats and proteins.

Ingredients

1 tablespoon of peanut butter,

1 sliced banana,

1 slice of whole wheat toast,

and a pinch of salt and pepper.

Process

a. Toast the slice of whole wheat bread, and then spread the tablespoon of peanut butter on top.

b. Slice the banana and add it on top of the toast.

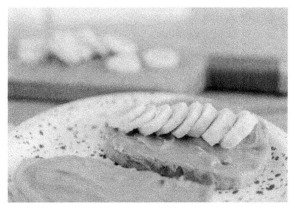

c. Sprinkle some salt and pepper on top if desired.

d. Enjoy.

Greek Yogurt Parfait

A Greek yogurt parfait is a great way to get some extra protein and fiber into your breakfast.

Ingredients

1 cup of Greek yogurt,

½ cup of granola, and

your favorite fruits.

Process

a. In a bowl, start by layering the Greek yogurt and granola.

b. Top it with your favorite fruits, such as blueberries, strawberries, or bananas.

c. Enjoy!

Blueberry Smoothie Bowl

A blueberry smoothie bowl is a great way to get some extra antioxidants and protein into your breakfast.

Ingredients

1 cup of frozen blueberries,

½ cup of unsweetened almond milk,

1 tablespoon of honey, and

your favorite toppings.

Process

a. Blend together the frozen blueberries, almond milk, and honey until smooth.

b. Pour the smoothie into a bowl and top it with your favorite toppings, such as chia seeds, sliced almonds, and dried coconut flakes.

c. Enjoy!

Egg and Cheese Sandwich

This classic egg and cheese sandwich is a great way to start your day with some extra protein.

Ingredients

2 eggs,

2 slices of whole wheat bread,

1 slice of cheese,

1 tablespoon of butter, and

a pinch of salt and pepper.

Process

a. Heat the butter in a pan over medium heat.

b. Whisk the eggs together with a pinch of salt and pepper, and then pour them into the pan.

c. Cook the eggs until they are almost done, and then add the slice of cheese to the pan.

d. Toast the two slices of whole wheat bread, and then top one slice with the egg and cheese.

e. Place the other slice of bread on top.

f. Enjoy.

Oatmeal with Berries

Oatmeal with berries is a great way to enjoy a healthy and filling breakfast.

Ingredients

½ cup of rolled oats,

1 cup of milk,

1 tablespoon of honey, and

½ cup of your favorite berries.

Process

a. In a pot, add the rolled oats and milk.

b. Cook over medium heat for about 5 minutes, until the oats are cooked through.

c. Stir in the honey, and then top with the berries.

d. Enjoy!

French Toast

French toast is a great way to start your day with some carbs and protein.

Ingredients

2 slices of whole wheat bread,

2 eggs,

2 tablespoons of milk,

1 tablespoon of butter,

1 teaspoon of cinnamon, and

a pinch of salt.

Process

a. In a bowl, whisk together the eggs, milk, cinnamon, and salt.

b. Heat the butter in a pan over medium heat.

c. Dip the slices of bread into the egg mixture and cook for about 2 minutes on each side.

d. Serve with your favorite toppings and enjoy! (Instead of cooking, you could also bake).

Baked Eggs in Avocado

Baked eggs in avocado is a great way to start your day with some healthy fats and protein.

Ingredients

1 avocado,

2 eggs,

1 tablespoon of olive oil, and

a pinch of salt and pepper.

Process

a. Preheat the oven to 375°F.

b. Cut the avocado in half and remove the pit.

c. Scoop out some of the avocado to make room for the eggs.

d. Place the avocado halves on a baking sheet and crack an egg into each one.

e. Drizzle with olive oil and season with salt and pepper.

f. Bake for about 10 minutes, or until the eggs are cooked to your liking.

g. Serve and enjoy!

Egg Muffins

Egg muffins are a great way to grab a healthy breakfast on the go.

Ingredients

6 eggs,

½ cup of shredded cheese,

1 cup of chopped vegetables, and

a pinch of salt and pepper.

Process

a. Preheat the oven to 375°F.

b. Grease a muffin tin with oil or butter.

c. In a bowl, whisk together the eggs, cheese, vegetables, salt, and pepper.

d. Pour the egg mixture into the muffin tin, filling each cup about ¾ of the way full.

e. Bake for about 15 minutes, or until the eggs are cooked through.

f. Serve and enjoy.

Breakfast Burrito

A breakfast burrito is a great way to start your day with some carbs, proteins, and healthy fats.

Ingredients

2 eggs,

1 tablespoon of olive oil,

1 whole wheat wrap,

½ cup of cooked black beans, and

your favorite toppings.

Process

a. Heat the olive oil in a pan over medium heat.

b. Whisk the eggs together with a pinch of salt and pepper, and then pour them into the pan.

c. Scramble the eggs until they are almost done, and then add the cooked black beans.

d. Spoon the egg and bean mixture onto the wrap, and then top with your favorite toppings.

e. Roll up the wrap and enjoy.

Protein Shake

A protein shake is a great way to get some extra protein into your breakfast.

Ingredients

1 scoop of protein powder,

1 cup of milk,

1 cup of frozen fruit, and

1 tablespoon of honey (optional).

Process

a. In a blender, combine the protein powder, milk, frozen fruit, and honey (if using).

b. Blend until smooth and enjoy.

Egg and Veggie Scramble

This egg and veggie scramble is a great way to start your day with some extra protein and fiber.

Ingredients

2 eggs,

1 tablespoon of olive oil,

1 cup of chopped vegetables, and

a pinch of salt and pepper.

Process

a. Heat the olive oil in a pan over medium heat.

b. Whisk the eggs together with a pinch of salt and pepper, and then pour them into the pan.

c. Scramble the eggs until they are almost done, and then add the chopped vegetables.

d. Stir everything together and cook for another few minutes, until the vegetables are cooked through.

e. Serve and enjoy.

Breakfast Quesadilla

A breakfast quesadilla is a great way to start your day with some carbs, proteins, and healthy fats.

Ingredients

2 eggs,

1 tablespoon of olive oil,

1 flour tortilla,

½ cup of shredded cheese, and

your favorite toppings.

Process

a. Heat the olive oil in a pan over medium heat.

b. Whisk the eggs together with a pinch of salt and pepper, and then pour them into the pan.

c. Scramble the eggs until they are almost done, and then add the shredded cheese.

d. Spoon the egg and cheese mixture onto one half of the tortilla, and then fold the other half over.

e. Cook for about 2 minutes on each side.

f. Slice into wedges, top with your favorite toppings, and enjoy.

Lunch Recipes for Healthy Weight Gain

Lentil Stew

A hearty, high-calorie stew that's packed with protein and fiber. Lentils are simmered in a flavorful broth with carrots, celery, onion, and garlic for a nutritious and filling meal.

Ingredients

1 cup dried lentils,

2 tablespoons olive oil,

1 onion, diced,

1 carrot, diced,

1 celery rib, diced,

2 cloves garlic, minced,

4 cups vegetable broth,

2 teaspoons dried thyme,

Salt and freshly ground black pepper, to taste.

Process

a. Heat oil in a large pot over medium heat.

b. Add onion, carrot and celery and cook, stirring occasionally, until vegetables are tender, about 8 minutes.

c. Add garlic and cook until fragrant, about 1 minute.

d. Add lentils, broth, and thyme.

e. Bring to a boil, reduce heat and simmer until lentils are tender, about 30 minutes.

f. Season with salt and pepper to taste.

Baked Sweet Potato Fries

Crispy, oven-baked sweet potato fries are a delicious way to add extra calories and nutrients to your diet.

Ingredients

2 large sweet potatoes, peeled and cut into wedges,

2 tablespoons olive oil,

2 teaspoons garlic powder,

1 teaspoon smoked paprika,

1 teaspoon cumin,

Salt and freshly ground black pepper, to taste.

Process

a. Preheat oven to 425°F.

b. Line a baking sheet with foil.

c. Place sweet potato wedges on prepared baking sheet.

d. Drizzle with olive oil and season with garlic powder, smoked paprika, cumin, salt, and pepper.

e. Toss to combine.

f. Bake for 15 minutes, then flip and bake for an additional 15 minutes, or until golden and crispy.

Egg Salad Sandwich

A high-calorie sandwich that's packed with protein and healthy fat.

Ingredients

4 hard-boiled eggs, chopped,

2 tablespoons mayonnaise,

2 tablespoons Dijon mustard,

2 tablespoons minced dill pickles,

Salt and freshly ground black pepper, to taste.

Process

a. In a medium bowl, combine chopped eggs, mayonnaise, mustard, and pickles.

b. Mix until combined.

c. Season with salt and pepper to taste.

d. Serve on toasted bread, or as desired.

Baked Potato Wedges

Crispy, oven-baked potato wedges are a delicious way to add extra calories to your diet.

Ingredients

4 large russet potatoes, cut into wedges,

2 tablespoons olive oil,

1 teaspoon garlic powder,

1 teaspoon smoked paprika,

Salt and freshly ground black pepper, to taste.

Process

a. Preheat oven to 425°F.

b. Line a baking sheet with foil.

c.   Place potato wedges on prepared baking sheet.

d.   Drizzle with olive oil and season with garlic powder, smoked paprika, salt and pepper.

e.   Toss to combine.

f.   Bake for 25 minutes, or until golden and crispy.

Sautéed Mushrooms and Onions

A delicious, high-calorie side dish that's full of protein and healthy fats.

Ingredients

2 tablespoons olive oil,

1 onion, sliced,

1 pound mushrooms, sliced,

2 cloves garlic, minced,

1 tablespoon fresh thyme leaves,

Salt and freshly ground black pepper, to taste.

Process

a. Heat oil in a large skillet over medium heat.

b. Add onion and cook, stirring occasionally, until softened, about 5 minutes.

c. Add mushrooms and cook, stirring occasionally, until softened and golden, about 10 minutes.

d. Add garlic and thyme and cook until fragrant, about 1 minute.

e. Season with salt and pepper to taste.

f. Enjoy!

Veggie and Hummus Wrap

A high calorie wrap that's packed with protein and healthy fats.

Ingredients

1 large wrap,

2 tablespoons hummus,

1/2 cup shredded carrots,

1/2 cup diced cucumber,

1/4 cup diced red onion,

Salt and freshly ground black pepper, to taste.

Process

a. Spread hummus in the center of the wrap.

b. Top with carrots, cucumber, and red onion.

c. Season with salt and pepper to taste.

d. Roll up and enjoy!

Lentil and Quinoa Bowl

A high-calorie bowl that's full of protein, fiber, and healthy fats.

Healthy Weight Gain

Ingredients

1/2 cup dry lentils,

1/2 cup dry quinoa,

2 cups vegetable broth,

1 teaspoon olive oil,

1 red bell pepper, diced,

1/2 onion, diced,

2 cloves garlic, minced,

Salt and freshly ground black pepper, to taste.

Process

a. In a medium saucepan, bring lentils, quinoa, and broth to a boil.

b. Reduce heat to low and simmer until lentils and quinoa are tender, about 20 minutes.

c. Heat oil in a large skillet over medium heat.

d. Add bell pepper, onion, and garlic and cook, stirring occasionally, until vegetables are tender, about 8 minutes.

e. Add cooked lentils and quinoa and stir to combine.

f. Season with salt and pepper to taste.

g. Enjoy!

Power Salad

A high-calorie salad that's packed with protein and healthy fats.

Ingredients

2 cups spinach,

1/2 cup cooked quinoa,

1/2 cup black beans,

1/4 cup diced red pepper,

1/4 cup diced red onion,

1/4 cup diced cucumber,

2 tablespoons olive oil,

2 tablespoons lemon juice,

Salt and freshly ground black pepper, to taste.

Process

a. In a large bowl, combine spinach, quinoa, black beans, red pepper, red onion, and cucumber.
b. Drizzle with olive oil and lemon juice and season with salt and pepper to taste.

c. Enjoy!

Baked Tofu

A high-calorie and protein-packed meal that's full of healthy fats.

Ingredients

1 package extra-firm tofu, cut into cubes,

2 tablespoons olive oil,

2 tablespoons soy sauce,

1 teaspoon garlic powder,

1 teaspoon smoked paprika,

Salt and freshly ground black pepper, to taste.

Process

a. Preheat oven to 425°F.

b. Line a baking sheet with foil.

c. Place tofu cubes on prepared baking sheet.

d. Drizzle with olive oil, soy sauce, garlic powder, and smoked paprika.

e. Toss to combine.

f. Bake for 25 minutes, or until golden and crispy.

g. Enjoy!

Lentil Pasta

A high-calorie and protein-packed meal that's full of complex carbs and fiber.

Ingredients

8 ounces lentil pasta,

2 tablespoons olive oil,

2 cloves garlic, minced,

1/4 cup diced onion,

1/4 cup diced red pepper,

1/4 cup diced tomatoes,

2 tablespoons tomato paste,

Salt and freshly ground black pepper, to taste.

Process

a. Cook pasta according to package instructions, drain and set aside.

b. Heat oil in a large skillet over medium heat.

c. Add garlic and onion and cook, stirring occasionally, until softened, about 5 minutes.

d. Add red pepper and cook until tender, about 5 minutes.

e. Add tomatoes, tomato paste, and cooked pasta and stir to combine.

f. Season with salt and pepper to taste.

g. Enjoy!

Quinoa Bowl

A hearty bowl of warm quinoa with vegetables and protein.

Ingredients

1 cup cooked quinoa,

2 tablespoons olive oil,

1/2 cup diced onion,

1/2 cup diced carrots,

1/2 cup diced red pepper,

2 cloves garlic, minced,

1 cup cooked black beans,

Salt and freshly ground black pepper, to taste.

Process

a. Heat oil in a large skillet over medium heat.

b. Add onion, carrots, and red pepper and cook, stirring occasionally, until softened, about 5 minutes.

c. Add garlic and cook until fragrant, about 1 minute.

d. Add black beans and cooked quinoa and stir to combine.

e. Season with salt and pepper to taste.

f. Enjoy!

Chickpea Salad

A protein-packed salad full of flavor and texture.

Ingredients

2 cups cooked chickpeas,

1/4 cup diced red onion,

1/4 cup diced cucumber,

1/4 cup diced tomatoes,

2 tablespoons chopped fresh parsley,

2 tablespoons olive oil,

2 tablespoons lemon juice,

Salt and freshly ground black pepper, to taste.

Process

a. In a large bowl, combine chickpeas, red onion, cucumber, tomatoes, and parsley.

b. In a small bowl, whisk together olive oil, lemon juice, salt, and pepper.

c. Pour dressing over salad and toss to combine.

d. Enjoy!

Veggie Wrap

A simple and delicious meal that's full of nutrition.

Ingredients

4 whole wheat wraps,

1/2 cup hummus,

1/2 cup diced red pepper,

1/2 cup diced cucumber,

1/2 cup diced tomatoes,

1/4 cup diced red onion,

2 tablespoons chopped fresh parsley.

Process

a. Spread hummus on wraps.

b. Top with red pepper, cucumber, tomatoes, red onion, and parsley.

c. Roll up wraps and enjoy!

Tuna Salad

A protein-packed salad that's full of flavor.

Ingredients

2 cans tuna, drained,

2 tablespoons mayonnaise,

2 tablespoons chopped celery,

2 tablespoons diced onion,

2 tablespoons sweet pickle relish,

Salt and freshly ground black pepper, to taste.

Process

a. In a medium bowl, combine tuna, mayonnaise, celery, onion, and pickle relish.

b. Season with salt and pepper to taste.

c. Serve on a bed of lettuce or with whole wheat crackers.

d. Enjoy!

Baked Salmon

A lean protein-packed meal that's full of healthy fats.

Ingredients

2 (6-ounce) salmon fillets,

2 tablespoons olive oil,

2 tablespoons freshly squeezed lemon juice,

2 cloves garlic, minced,

Salt and freshly ground black pepper, to taste.

Process

a. Preheat oven to 375°F.

b. Grease a baking dish.

c. Place salmon fillets in the prepared dish and brush with olive oil.

d. Sprinkle with lemon juice, garlic, salt, and pepper.

e. Bake for 15-20 minutes, or until fish is cooked through.

f. Enjoy!

Dinner Recipes for Healthy Weight Gain

Spinach and Ricotta Stuffed Shells

These cheesy shells are a delicious way to get in extra calories without feeling heavy.

Ingredients

Jumbo pasta shells

Ricotta cheese

Spinach

Parmesan cheese

Marinara sauce

Process

a.   Preheat oven to 375°F.

b.   Boil the jumbo pasta shells according to package instructions.

c.   Mix the ricotta, spinach, and Parmesan cheese together in a bowl.

d.   Stuff each shell with the ricotta mixture.

e.   Place the stuffed shells in a baking dish and top with marinara sauce.

f.   Bake for 30 minutes.

Beef and Broccoli Stir Fry

Ingredients

Beef

Broccoli

Garlic

Ginger

Oil

Rice

Process

a.   Heat oil in a wok or skillet over medium-high heat.

b.   Add the beef and cook for 2-3 minutes, stirring occasionally.

c.   Add the broccoli, garlic and ginger and cook for an additional 3-4 minutes.

d.   Serve over cooked rice.

Baked Potato with Cheese and Bacon

This is a great comfort food and an easy way to add extra calories.

Ingredients

Potato

Cheese

Bacon

Green onion

Process

a.   Preheat oven to 400°F.

b. Wash and pat dry the potato.

c. Prick the potato with a fork several times.

d. Place the potato on a baking sheet and bake for 45-50 minutes.

e. Remove the potato from the oven, slice it open and top with cheese, bacon, and green onion.

f. Serve.

Salmon and Asparagus Bake

This is a great way to get in extra calories and nutrients with a piece of salmon.

Ingredients

Salmon

Asparagus

Parmesan cheese

Olive oil

Process

a. Preheat oven to 375°F.

b. Place the salmon on a baking sheet.

c.   Top the salmon with asparagus, Parmesan cheese and olive oil.

d.   Bake for 20 minutes.

Mac and Cheese Bake

Ingredients

Macaroni

Cheese

Butter

Milk

Breadcrumbs

Process

a.   Preheat oven to 375°F.

b.   Cook macaroni according to package instructions.

c.   Mix the cooked macaroni with cheese, butter, and milk.

d.   Place the macaroni in a baking dish and top with breadcrumbs.

e.   Bake for 20 minutes.

Chicken and Rice Casserole

Ingredients

Chicken

Rice

Vegetables

Cheese

Breadcrumbs

Process

a. Preheat oven to 375°F.

b. Mix cooked chicken, rice, vegetables, and cheese together in a bowl.

c. Place the mixture in a baking dish and top with breadcrumbs.

d. Bake for 20 minutes.

Lasagna

Lasagna is a classic Italian dish that is full of flavor and calories.

Ingredients

Lasagna noodles

Ricotta cheese

Mozzarella cheese

Marinara sauce

Process

a. Preheat oven to 375°F.

b. Layer lasagna noodles in a baking dish.

c. Spread ricotta cheese over the noodles.

d. Top with mozzarella cheese and marinara sauce.

e. Bake for 30 minutes.

Baked Ziti

A delicious Italian dish that will add calories to your diet.

Ingredients

Ziti

Ricotta

Mozzarella and Parmesan cheese

Marinara sauce

Process

a. Preheat oven to 375°F.

b. Cook ziti according to package instruction.

c. Mix the ziti with ricotta, mozzarella, and Parmesan cheese.

d. Place the ziti in a baking dish and top with marinara sauce.

e. Bake for 30 minutes.

Sweet Potato Pie

Ingredients

Sweet potato

Butter

Sugar

Cinnamon

Pie crust

Process

a. Preheat oven to 375°F.

b. Bake the sweet potato for 45 minutes.

c. Mash the sweet potato with butter, sugar, and cinnamon.

d. Place the mixture in a pie crust.

e. Bake for 30 minutes.

Quinoa Bowl

Ingredients

Quinoa

Vegetables

Nuts

Cheese

Avocado

Process

a. Cook quinoa according to package instructions.

b. Place the quinoa in a bowl and top with vegetables, nuts, cheese and avocado.

c. Serve.

Shepherd's Pie

A hearty and filling dish that will give you all the extra calories you need.

Ingredients

Ground beef

Vegetables

Mashed potatoes

Process

a. Preheat oven to 375°F.

b. Layer cooked ground beef and vegetables in a baking dish.

c. Top with mashed potatoes.

d. Bake for 30 minutes.

Vegetable Frittata

Ingredients

Vegetables

Eggs

Process

a. Preheat oven to 375°F.

b. Sauté the vegetables in a pan.

c. Mix the vegetables with eggs.

d. Place the mixture in a baking dish and bake for 30 minutes.

Stuffed Peppers

Ingredients

Bell peppers

Ground beef

Rice

Vegetables

Process

a. Preheat oven to 375°F.

b. Cook the ground beef, rice, and vegetables in a pan.

c. Stuff the peppers with the mixture.

d. Place the peppers in a baking dish and bake for 25 minutes.

Baked Chicken Parmesan

Ingredients

Chicken breasts

Breadcrumbs

Marinara sauce

Cheese

Process

a. Preheat oven to 375°F.

b. Bread the chicken breasts.

c. Place the chicken in a baking dish and top with marinara sauce and cheese.

d. Bake for 30 minutes or until golden brown.

Baked Salmon with Vegetables

Salmon is a great source of healthy fats and calories.

Ingredients

Salmon fillets

Vegetables

Olive oil

Process

a. Preheat oven to 375°F.

b. Place the salmon fillets and vegetables on a baking sheet.

c. Top with olive oil and bake for 15 minutes.

Beef Stroganoff

Ingredients

Mushrooms

Onions

Ground beef

Sour cream

Egg noodles

Process

a. Sauté the mushrooms and onions in a pan.

b. Add the ground beef and cook until browned.

c. Stir in the sour cream and heat until bubbling.

d. Serve over cooked egg noodles.

Chicken Pot Pie

Ingredients

Pie crust

Chicken

Vegetables

Gravy

Process

a. Preheat oven to 375°F.

b. Layer the chicken, vegetables, and gravy in the pie crust.

c. Bake for 25 minutes or until golden brown.

Chili and Rice

A hearty and filling dish that will give you extra calories.

Ingredients

Chili

Rice

Process

a. Cook the chili in a pot.

b. Cook the rice according to package directions.

c. Serve the chili over the cooked rice.

Fish Tacos

Ingredients

Fish

Vegetables

Cheese

Tortillas

Process

a. Grill the fish.

b. Top the fish with vegetables and cheese.

c. Serve in a tortilla.

Baked Cheese Ravioli

A delicious Italian dish that is full of flavor and calories.

Ingredients

Cheese ravioli

Marinara sauce

Cheese

Process

Healthy Weight Gain

a. Preheat oven to 375°F.

b. Layer the ravioli, sauce, and cheese in a baking dish.

c. Bake for 25 minutes or until golden brown.

CHAPTER 3

THE RIGHT WAY TO SNACKING FOR HEALTHY WEIGHT GAIN

Snacking is an effective strategy to support healthy weight gain, as it can help to increase overall calorie intake throughout the day and provide your body with the nutrients it needs. When choosing snacks for weight gain, it's important to focus on calorie-dense options that provide a good balance of carbohydrates, protein, and healthy fats.

Some examples of healthy snacks for weight gain include:

1. Nuts and nut butter: Nuts and nut butter are a great source of healthy fats, protein, and fiber. They are also calorie-dense, making them an ideal snack for weight gain. Consider snacking on almonds, cashews, peanut butter, or almond butter.
2. Greek yogurt: Greek yogurt is a great source of protein, which can help to support muscle growth and weight gain. It also provides calcium and other important nutrients.

Consider topping Greek yogurt with fruit or granola for added flavor and nutrition.

3. Avocado: Make avocado your best friend as it is a great source of healthy fats, fiber, and a range of vitamins and minerals. Consider snacking on avocado toast or using avocado as a dip for vegetables.

4. Dried fruit: Dried fruit is a calorie-dense snack that provides a good balance of carbohydrates and fiber. It's important to choose varieties without added sugar and to consume in moderation due to their high sugar content.

5. Hummus and vegetables: Hummus is a great source of protein and healthy fats, and pairs well with raw vegetables such as carrots, celery, and bell peppers.

When snacking for weight gain, it's important to avoid high-sugar and high-fat options that can contribute to excess calorie intake and negatively impact health. Additionally, it's important to consume snacks in moderation and to balance them with regular meals and exercise to support overall health and weight gain efforts.

Snacking on Healthy Sweets and Desserts (20 recipes for weight gain)

Oatmeal Raisin Cookies

Soft and chewy oatmeal cookies loaded with raisins and brown sugar for a classic snack.

Ingredients

2 1/4 cups all-purpose flour

1 teaspoon baking soda

1 teaspoon ground cinnamon

1/2 teaspoon salt

1 cup (2 sticks) butter, softened.

1 cup granulated sugar.

1 cup packed light-brown sugar

2 large eggs

1 teaspoon vanilla extract

3 cups rolled oats.

1 cup raisins

Process

1. Preheat oven to 350 degrees F.

2. In a medium bowl, whisk together the flour, baking soda, cinnamon, and salt.

3. In a separate bowl, cream together the butter and both sugars until light and fluffy.

4. Beat in the eggs one at a time.

5. Stir in the vanilla.

6. Gradually add the flour mixture, stirring until just combined.

7. Stir in the oatmeal and raisins until evenly distributed.

8. Drop tablespoons of dough onto ungreased baking sheets.

9. Bake for 10 to 12 minutes, or until golden brown.

10. Let cool on the baking sheet for 2 minutes before transferring to a wire rack to cool completely.

Almond Butter Banana Roll-Ups

A healthy, protein-packed snack made with almond butter, banana, and honey.

Ingredients

- 1 whole-wheat tortilla
- 2 tablespoons almond butter
- 1 banana, sliced
- 1 tablespoon honey

Process

1. Spread the almond butter onto the tortilla.
2. Arrange the banana slices on top of the almond butter.
3. Drizzle with honey.
4. Roll up the tortilla tightly and cut into slices.

5. Serve immediately.

Peanut Butter Energy Balls

Protein-packed peanut butter balls made with oats and honey.

Ingredients
- 1 cup rolled oats
- 1/4 cup honey
- 1/4 cup peanut butter
- 2 tablespoons ground flaxseed
- 2 tablespoons dark chocolate chips

Process
1. In a medium bowl, mix the oats, honey, peanut butter, and flaxseed until combined.
2. Stir in the chocolate chips.
3. Roll the mixture into small balls.
4. Place the balls on a baking sheet lined with parchment paper.
5. Refrigerate for at least one hour before serving.

Trail Mix

A delicious and nutritious snack made with a variety of nuts, seeds, and dried fruit.

Ingredients
- 1/2 cup almonds
- 1/4 cup walnuts
- 1/4 cup sunflower seeds
- 1/4 cup pumpkin seeds
- 1/4 cup raisins
- 1/4 cup dried cranberries
- 1/4 cup dark chocolate chips

Process
1. In a large bowl, mix all the ingredients.
2. Store in an airtight container in the pantry or refrigerator.
3. Enjoy!

Sweet Potato Fries

Delicious oven-baked sweet potato fries with a hint of cinnamon.

Ingredients

• 2 large sweet potatoes, peeled and cut into strips
• 2 tablespoons olive oil
• 1 teaspoon ground cinnamon
• Salt and pepper, to taste

Process

1. Preheat oven to 425 degrees F.
2. Place the sweet potato strips onto a baking sheet and drizzle with olive oil.
3. Sprinkle with cinnamon, salt, and pepper.
4. Bake for 15 to 20 minutes, flipping halfway through.
5. Serve warm.

Protein Smoothie

A creamy and nutritious smoothie made with yogurt, peanut butter, and banana.

Ingredients
- 1/2 cup plain Greek yogurt
- 1/4 cup milk
- 1 tablespoon peanut butter
- 1 banana
- 1 tablespoon honey

Process
1. Place all the ingredients in a blender and blend until smooth.
2. Pour into a glass and enjoy!

Chocolate Avocado Pudding

A creamy and delicious pudding made with avocado, cocoa powder, and honey.

Ingredients

- 2 ripe avocados, peeled and pitted
- 1/4 cup cocoa powder
- 1/4 cup honey
- 1 teaspoon vanilla extract
- Pinch of salt

Process

1. Place the avocados, cocoa powder, honey, vanilla, and salt in a food processor and blend until smooth.
2. Serve chilled.

Cheese and Fruit Plate

A tasty and nutritious snack plate made with cheese, fresh fruit, and crackers.

Ingredients

- 1/2 cup cubed cheese
- 1/2 cup grapes
- 1/2 cup sliced apples
- 1/2 cup sliced pears
- 1/2 cup crackers

Process

1. Arrange the cheese, grapes, apples, and pears on a plate.
2. Serve with crackers.
3. Enjoy!

Banana Bread

A moist and delicious banana bread made with mashed bananas and walnuts.

Ingredients

- 1 1/2 cups all-purpose flour
- 1 teaspoon baking soda
- 1 teaspoon ground cinnamon
- 1/4 teaspoon salt
- 2 large ripe bananas, mashed

- 1/3 cup melted butter
- 1/2 cup packed brown sugar
- 1/4 cup granulated sugar
- 1 large egg
- 1 teaspoon vanilla extract
- 1/2 cup chopped walnuts

Process

1. Preheat oven to 350 degrees F. Grease a 9x5 inch loaf pan.

2. In a medium bowl, whisk together the flour, baking soda, cinnamon, and salt.

3. In a separate bowl, cream together the butter and both sugars until light and fluffy.

4. Beat in the egg and vanilla.

5. Gradually add the flour mixture to the butter mixture, stirring until just combined.

6. Stir in the mashed bananas and walnuts.

7. Pour the batter into the prepared pan and bake for 50 to 60 minutes, or until a toothpick inserted into the center comes out clean.

8. Let cool in the pan for 10 minutes before transferring to a wire rack to cool completely.

Popcorn

A light and tasty snack made with air-popped popcorn and your favorite seasonings.

Ingredients

- 1/2 cup popcorn kernels
- 2 tablespoons vegetable oil
- Salt and pepper, to taste.

Process

1. Heat the oil in a large pot over medium-high heat.

2. Add the popcorn kernels and cover with a lid.

3. Shake the pot occasionally to prevent the popcorn from burning.

4. Once the popping has slowed down, remove the pot from the heat and season with salt and pepper.

5. Serve warm.

Peanut Butter Protein Balls

An easy and delicious snack packed with protein and fiber.

Ingredients

- 1 cup peanut butter
- 1 cup rolled oats
- 1/2 cup honey
- 1/2 cup ground flaxseed
- 1/3 cup raisins
- 1/3 cup chopped walnuts

Process

1. In a medium bowl, combine the peanut butter, oats, honey, flaxseed, raisins, and walnuts.

2. Mix until well combined.

3. Roll the mixture into small balls and place on a baking sheet.

4. Place in the refrigerator for at least an hour to firm up.

5. Serve chilled.

Trail Mix

A delicious and nutritious snack packed with protein, fiber, and healthy fats.

Ingredients
- 1 cup nuts of your choice
- 1 cup dried fruits of your choice
- 1 cup seeds of your choice
- 1/2 cup dark chocolate chips (optional)

Process
1. In a medium bowl, combine the nuts, dried fruits, and seeds.
2. Add the dark chocolate chips, if desired.
3. Mix until well combined.
4. Store in an airtight container.
5. Enjoy!

Apple Nachos

Sweet and crunchy apple nachos that are sure to satisfy.

Ingredients

- 1 large apple, thinly sliced
- 1/4 cup peanut butter
- 1/4 cup chocolate chips
- 1/4 cup chopped nuts
- 1/4 cup shredded coconut
- 1 tablespoon honey

Process

1. Arrange the apple slices on a plate.
2. In a small bowl, melt the peanut butter in the microwave.
3. Drizzle the melted peanut butter over the apple slices.
4. Top with the chocolate chips, nuts, and coconut.
5. Drizzle with honey.
6. Serve immediately.

Greek Yogurt with Berries

A creamy and delicious snack made with Greek yogurt and fresh berries.

Ingredients

- 1 cup Greek yogurt
- 1/2 cup fresh berries of your choice
- 2 tablespoons chopped nuts
- 2 tablespoons honey

Process

1. In a bowl, combine the yogurt, berries, and nuts.
2. Drizzle with honey.
3. Enjoy!

Edamame

A simple and nutritious snack that is full of protein and fiber.

Ingredients

- 1 cup frozen edamame
- 1 tablespoon olive oil
- 1 teaspoon garlic powder

• 1/2 teaspoon salt

Process

1. Heat the olive oil in a skillet over medium-high heat.

2. Add the edamame and season with garlic powder and salt.

3. Cook for 5-7 minutes, stirring occasionally.

4. Serve warm.

Baked Apples

A sweet and comforting snack made with apples and your favorite spices.

Ingredients

• 2 apples, cored and thinly sliced

• 2 tablespoons butter

• 2 tablespoons brown sugar

• 1 teaspoon cinnamon

• 1/2 teaspoon nutmeg

• 1/4 teaspoon allspice

• 1/4 cup raisins (optional).

Process

1. Preheat oven to 375 degrees F.

2. Place the apple slices in a baking dish.

3. Dot with butter and sprinkle with brown sugar, cinnamon, nutmeg, and allspice.

4. Add the raisins, if desired.

5. Bake for 20-25 minutes, or until apples are tender.

6. Serve warm.

Chocolate Banana Smoothie

A creamy and decadent smoothie made with banana, almond milk, and cocoa powder.

Ingredients

- 1 ripe banana
- 1 cup almond milk
- 2 tablespoons cocoa powder
- 1 teaspoon honey (optional)
- Ice cubes (optional)

Process

1. Peel and slice the banana.

2. Place the banana in a blender and add the almond milk, cocoa powder, and honey (if using).

3. Blend until smooth.

4. Add ice cubes if desired.

5. Serve chilled.

Chocolate Coconut Bites

Delicious and sweet treats made with coconut, chocolate, and nuts.

Ingredients

• 1 cup shredded coconut

• ¼ cup cocoa powder

• ½ cup chopped nuts (almonds, walnuts, etc.)

• 2 tablespoons honey

• 1 teaspoon vanilla extract

Process

1. In a large bowl, combine the shredded coconut, cocoa powder, and chopped nuts.

2. Add the honey and vanilla extract and mix until everything is well combined.

3. Form the mixture into bite-sized pieces and place on a baking sheet.

4. Refrigerate for at least one hour before serving.

Salmon Cakes

Delicious and high-calorie salmon cakes that are packed with protein and healthy fats.

Ingredients

- 2 cans salmon, drained and flaked.
- 2 eggs
- 2 tablespoons Dijon mustard
- 1/2 cup breadcrumbs
- 1/4 cup minced onion.
- 1/4 cup minced fresh parsley.
- Salt and freshly ground black pepper, to taste.

Process

1. In a medium bowl, combine salmon, eggs, mustard, breadcrumbs, onion, and parsley. Mix until combined.
2. Season with salt and pepper to taste.
3. Form into patties.
4. Heat a large skillet over medium heat.
5. Add salmon patties and cook until golden and cooked through, about 8 minutes per side.
6. Enjoy!

CHAPTER 4

SLEEPING FOR WEIGHT GAIN

Sleep is a crucial component of your weight gain journey and an important part of a healthy lifestyle. It is however, often overlooked. The quality of your sleep plays a vital role in your overall health and wellbeing, including the ability to gain weight. You should aim for seven to eight hours of sleep per night to support healthy weight gain.

In this chapter, I will explore the importance of sleep for weight gain and provide tips on how to improve sleep quality.

How Sleep Affects Weight Gain

First, sleep deprivation disrupts the body's natural hormone production, including growth hormone, which is essential for building muscle mass. This is also important because the reparation of the muscles you have targeted with exercise happens when you sleep.

Healthy Weight Gain

Getting enough sleep can help to regulate your hormones, which can help to increase your appetite and thus increase your calorie intake.

We discussed metabolism earlier; sleep is also a key factor that affects metabolism. During sleep, the body undergoes important metabolic processes that are essential for regulating appetite and burning calories. Without enough sleep, these processes are disrupted. Getting enough sleep can help to ensure that your body has the energy it needs to support your weight gain goals.

Sleep can also help to reduce stress and improve your overall mental health.

Tips for Improving Sleep Quality

Getting enough sleep can be challenging, but there are a few things that you can do to help ensure that you are getting enough rest:

- ✓ Stick to a consistent sleep schedule. Try to go to bed and wake up at the same time every day, even on weekends.

- ✓ Create a sleep-conducive environment. Make sure your bedroom is quiet, cool, and dark, and use comfortable bedding and pillows.
- ✓ Limit screen time before bed. Blue light emitted by electronic devices can disrupt sleep patterns, so try to avoid using screens for at least an hour before bed.
- ✓ Establish a relaxing bedtime routine. This can include activities such as reading, listening to calming music, or taking a warm bath.
- ✓ Avoid caffeine and alcohol before bedtime. These substances can disrupt sleep patterns and make it harder to fall and stay asleep.
- ✓ Exercise regularly. Regular exercise can help improve sleep quality but be sure to finish exercising at least a few hours before bedtime.

P.S: These tips also help if you're perchance an insomniac.

In conclusion, sleep is a crucial factor in weight gain and overall health. By prioritizing sleep and making small changes to improve sleep quality, you improve your ability to gain weight and build muscle mass.

Healthy Weight Gain

Getting enough sleep is just as important as proper nutrition and exercise in achieving weight gain goals, and should not be overlooked.

CHAPTER 5

EXERCISING FOR WEIGHT GAIN

This is the third leg of the Eat-Sleep-Exercise approach to weight gain. Exercise plays a role in gaining weight even as an underweight or skinny person. Exercising regularly can help you build muscle mass, increase your appetite, and improve your overall health.

Here's a heads up: whether you choose to hit the gym or workout from home, you will get a lot of "but why are you exercising?" You may respond, or not- you are doing this for you, no one else.

While many people associate exercise with weight loss, it can actually be used to help you gain and maintain a healthy weight. Exercise can help you to build muscle, which in turn can help you to gain weight, as well as helping you to increase your metabolism. In addition to consuming more calories, it's important to engage in regular exercise to promote muscle growth. Muscle tissue is more metabolically active than fat tissue, meaning that it burns more calories at rest. Therefore, building muscle through resistance training can help increase your overall calorie burn and support healthy weight gain, making you look and feel better. It also helps to regulate hormones and improve overall health.

In this chapter, we will explore different types of exercises that are ideal for weight gain and provide tips on how to safely incorporate exercise into your daily routine.

Ideal Exercises for Weight Gain

I.   Strength Training

While cardiovascular exercise is important for overall health, strength training can help build muscle mass and promote weight gain. Strength training is the most effective way to gain weight and build muscle mass. Resistance training stimulates muscle growth by creating small tears in muscle fibers, which then repair and grow stronger with proper nutrition and rest. It's important to progressively overload your muscles by increasing the weight or resistance over time to continue making gains. Exercises such as weightlifting, push-ups, and squats can help increase muscle mass and support healthy weight gain.

There are several different types of strength training exercises you can do, including:

1. Compound Exercises: Compound exercises are exercises that work multiple muscle groups at once, such as squats, deadlifts, and bench presses. These exercises are great for building overall muscle mass and strength.

2. Isolation Exercises: Isolation exercises are exercises that target specific muscle groups, such as bicep curls or triceps extensions. These exercises can be useful for targeting weaker or less developed muscles.

3. Bodyweight Exercises: Bodyweight exercises, such as push-ups and pull-ups, are great for beginners or for those who don't have access to a gym. These exercises can also be done anywhere, making them a convenient option for those with busy schedules.

II.   Cardiovascular Exercise

While strength training is the most effective way to gain weight, cardiovascular exercise can also be beneficial for weight gain. Cardiovascular exercise can help increase your appetite, improve your heart health, and reduce stress levels.

Some examples of cardiovascular exercises include:

1. Running or Jogging: Running or jogging is a great way to burn calories and improve your cardiovascular health.

2. Cycling: Cycling is a low-impact exercise that can help you burn calories and improve your cardiovascular health.

3. Swimming: Swimming is a great full-body workout that can help you burn calories and build endurance.

4. High-Intensity Interval Training (HIIT): HIIT workouts are short, intense workouts that can help you burn calories and improve your cardiovascular health.

III.   Flexibility Exercises

Flexibility exercises are a type of exercise that can help to improve your range of motion. They can also help to reduce stress and improve your overall health.

Examples of flexibility exercises include yoga, stretching, and Pilates.

Exercise For Weight Gain Without Equipment

Gaining weight and building muscle doesn't necessarily require access to a gym or expensive equipment. I didn't have to hit the gym. There are many bodyweight exercises that can be done at home or in a park that are effective for building strength and muscle mass.

Here are some bodyweight exercises for weight gain without equipment:

➤ Push-ups: Push-ups are a great exercise for building chest, shoulder, and triceps muscles. They can be done in variations to target different muscle groups, such as diamond push-ups, wide push-ups, and decline push-ups.

➤ Squats: Squats are a great exercise for building leg muscles, including quads, hamstrings, and glutes. They can be done with or without added weight, such as a backpack filled with books or water bottles.

➢ Lunges: Lunges are another exercise that targets the legs and glutes. They can be done in variations, such as forward lunges, backward lunges, curtsy lunges and side lunges.

➢ Dips: Dips are a great exercise for building triceps and chest muscles. They can be done on a bench, chair, or even the edge of a bathtub.

➢ Planks: Planks are an effective exercise for building core strength and stability. They can be done in variations, such as side planks and plank jacks, to target different areas of the core.

➢ Pull-ups: Pull-ups are a great exercise for building back and arm muscles. They can be done using a tree branch or playground equipment, or even a sturdy door frame pull-up bar.

➢ Burpees: Burpees are a full-body exercise that combines squats, push-ups, and jumps. They are great for building endurance and increasing heart rate.

Healthy Weight Gain

Incorporating these bodyweight exercises into a regular routine can help build muscle mass and improve overall fitness. It's important to challenge yourself and track progress over time to continue to see results. Again, proper nutrition and rest are essential for weight gain and muscle growth.

Other exercises include:

1. Squats
2. Deadlifts
3. Bench press
4. Lunges
5. Shoulder press
6. Pullups
7. Pushups
8. Bent-over rows
9. Dips
10. Bicep curls
11. Triceps extensions
12. Step-ups
13. Hip thrusts
14. Leg press

15. Calf raises

16. Reverse crunches

17. Planks

18. Burpees

19. Jumping jacks

20. Mountain climbers

Tips for Exercising for Weight Gain

✓ Be consistent: Consistency is key when it comes to exercising for weight gain. Aim to exercise at least three to four times per week to see results.

✓ Track your progress: Keep a log of your workouts and track your progress over time. This will help you see how far you've come and motivate you to continue making progress. There are workout apps you can use to make this easier.

✓ Focus on form: Proper form is essential for getting the most out of your workouts and avoiding injuries. If you're not sure how to perform an exercise correctly, ask a trainer or watch instructional videos online.

- ✓ Don't overdo it: While it's important to challenge yourself, it's also important to listen to your body and avoid overtraining. If you're feeling excessively sore or fatigued, take a break and rest.
- ✓ Fuel your body: Proper nutrition is essential for gaining weight and building muscle mass. Make sure to eat a balanced diet that includes plenty of protein, carbohydrates, and healthy fats.
- ✓ Hydrate: It is important to drink plenty of water throughout your exercise routine and to wear the appropriate clothing and safety gear. Finally, it is important to and take breaks when needed.

Overall, incorporating exercise into your weight gain program can help you achieve your goals and improve your overall health. Exercising regularly is essential for weight gain and building muscle mass. Strength training is the most effective way to gain weight, but cardiovascular exercise can also be beneficial. By being consistent, tracking your progress, focusing on form, avoiding overtraining, and fueling your body with proper nutrition, you can build muscle mass and improve your overall fitness. Gaining weight can be a slow process, therefore, be patient. Finally,

Healthy Weight Gain

it is important to focus on quality over quantity when it comes to exercise, as doing too much exercise can actually lead to weight loss.

CHAPTER 6

LIVING YOUR BEST LIFE

In this book, we've covered a variety of topics related to weight gain, including the importance of nutrition, exercise, and lifestyle factors. We've discussed the best foods to eat for weight gain, how to design a meal plan, and the importance of tracking progress. We've also covered exercises for weight gain and the importance of rest and recovery. We've addressed common obstacles and myths related to weight gain, such as the belief that gaining weight is unhealthy or that certain body types are unable to gain weight. Everybody can gain weight, healthily, if they put their minds to it.

Gaining weight in a healthy way can be a challenging process, but not impossible. With the proper guidance and dedication, it can be done successfully. Your body goal is an achievable goal, but it is important to take a balanced and thoughtful approach. Exercise can be an effective tool for gaining weight, but it is important to do it safely.

Healthy Weight Gain

There are many different types of exercise for weight gain, including strength training, cardiovascular exercise, and flexibility exercises. Eating a healthy, balanced diet is also essential for gaining weight, as it can help to ensure that you are getting the necessary nutrients and calories to support your body.

In addition to nutrition and exercise, lifestyle factors such as stress management and sleep can also impact weight gain. Stress can lead to increased cortisol levels, which can interfere with weight gain. Practicing stress-reducing techniques such as meditation, yoga, or deep breathing can help manage stress levels.

Focus on sustainable habits and to be patient, as weight gain is a slow and gradual process. Gaining weight requires commitment, patience, and perseverance. It's important to remember that weight gain is not just about increasing numbers on a scale, but about improving overall health and wellbeing. While it can be tempting to rely on quick fixes or extreme methods, the most effective approach is a sustainable one that incorporates healthy habits and balanced nutrition.

Healthy Weight Gain

With the right mindset and approach, you can achieve your weight gain goals and improve your overall health and happiness. The truth is that once you imbibe healthy habits as we discussed in this book, maintaining the weight you have gained becomes easy. Your body will thank you for it.

If you have medical issues, please consult with your healthcare provider before starting a weight gain program to ensure that it's safe and appropriate for you.

Maddie's journey had been challenging, but it had also been transformative. She had gone from a place of darkness, insecurity, and despair to a place of light, confidence and hope. And she knew that she was capable of achieving anything she set her mind to, as long as she had the courage and determination to keep going...

www.ingramcontent.com/pod-product-compliance
Lightning Source LLC
La Vergne TN
LVHW011926110325
805711LV00008B/405